Baptism

Three aspects
- archaelogical
- historical
- biblical

by F. M. Buhler

Translated by W. P. Bauman

Foreword by Michael A. G. Haykin

joshua
press

Joshua Press Inc., Dundas, Ontario, Canada
www.joshuapress.com

National Library of Canada Cataloguing in Publication Data available

ISBN 1-894400-20-8

Printed in Canada by Britannia Printers, 138 Main Street, Toronto, ON M4E 2V8
Binding courtesy of Holmes The Finishing House, 200 Ferrier, Markham, ON L3R 2Z5

CONTENTS

SECOND SECTION:
Biblical aspects of baptism, return to the sources

FOREWORD
By Dr Michael A.G. Haykin

In the modern English-speaking world, it was the Baptists who were the first to rediscover the biblical position on baptism, namely, that the Scriptures sanction the baptism of believers only. Since the emergence of the Baptist testimony in the British Isles in the seventeenth century, Baptists have written much on this important subject. What gives this work by Professor Buhler a somewhat unique quality is his deep knowledge of the archaeology of early baptisteries that has been gained on the field in archaeological digs. As he amply shows, the historical development of these baptisteries — from larger pools that could accommodate the immersion of baptismal candidates to much smaller fonts — reveals a movement away from the biblical understanding of baptism.

Originally written in French, it is a privilege and a joy to recommend this book now to a wider audience in the Anglophone world. Its thesis deserves serious consideration. Inasmuch as I am currently the Principal of Toronto Baptist Seminary, it is also a pleasure to commend this book by one of the early alumni of this school. His life and words touched many when he was at the school in the 1930s — as has his witness down through the years. May this book be used by God to speak to numerous others and so shed light for them on this important subject of baptism.

Dundas, Ontario
April 26, 2004

PREFACE
F.M. Buhler

The long history of baptism shows a constant development of the teaching of the Lord and his apostles. The changes or innovations which this ordinance experienced from the 1st and 2nd centuries of our era, made of baptism by immersion, conferred only on repentant sinners believing in Christ, a sacrament administered to infants, supposing to accomplish that which was to be symbolized.

This evolution is very visible through the baptismal installations, which in the course of centuries underwent progressive shrinking. In a parallel direction one can observe, on the doctrinal plane, a substitution of the sacrament for the symbol. Archaeology and the history of the Church witness in like manner a real deviation.

The work presented here has to do essentially with the Mediterranean basin, cradle of primitive and authentic Christianity, which conceals so many traces of baptismal practices which are according to Scripture.

I express my profound gratitude to the translator, Wilfred Bauman, a friend of many years (since 1933) who was interested in the French version of this work. Now it is the English translation which makes this material accessible to the English speaking world, especially American and British. I wish to heartily thank all those who have availed themselves of this material and have broadcast this little book, which is only the summary of the knowledge acquired by the author on this subject since 1960.

I sincerely desire that God may use it for His glory.

Mulhouse
October 15, 2003

6

FIRST SECTION

ARCHAEOLOGICAL AND
HISTORICAL ASPECTS

ARCHAEOLOGICAL AND HISTORICAL ASPECTS

INTRODUCTION

In this study, we are led to appeal jointly or successively to archaeology, history and theology.

After briefly describing Christianity of the first century, we will examine in turn three principal epochs in the course of which notable changes took place. Our outline then is this:

1. The period of the primitive church: 1st century;

2. The period of the first innovations: 2nd and 3rd centuries;

3. The period of the radical transformation of Christianity: 4th century;

4. The period during which the changes are defined and consolidated: beginning in the 5th century.

1. THE PERIOD OF THE PRIMITIVE CHURCH: FIRST CENTURY

The sources

For the initial phase, we essentially depend on writings of the apostles or their close collaborators, gathered together into one collection called the New Testament, which constitutes the basis of our Christian confessions. These texts are authoritative. There is relatively little difference between the editing and the events which they report. Further, they have been recopied with great care. There exist numerous copies[1] of which the most ancient are close to the originals. Moreover, we have at our disposal translations[2] which go back further in which there are variations that have to do with spelling, grammar or efforts of harmonization, without notable changes as to the meaning of the text.

Besides, the cross-checking between the various texts at our disposal, in the original language or in the translations, permits the specialists in textual criticism[3] to choose the most probable lesson[4], so that we can resort to these precious texts without risking an error as to the facts reported or the thoughts expressed by Jesus Christ or His apostles.

The character of biblical Christianity

On the basis of these documents, it is of extreme importance for our discourse to establish the nature of original Christianity. It has to do, in fact, with the point of departure

---

[1]   More than 200 uncial manuscripts (upper case) and about 6,000 cursive (lower case) of the New Testament.

[2]   Diverse translations of the Bible according to Hebrew and Greek texts.

[3]   M.J. Lagrange, *La Critique Textuelle*, Paris 1935.

[4]   See Glossary.

and the long evolution of theology and by way of consequence, the practice of baptism throughout the ages. It is this practice which determined the configuration and the dimensions of baptismal installations of which we have found here and there archaeological remains.

Religion of salvation

From the beginning Christianity is essentially a religion of salvation (1 Tim. 2:4). This salvation, with its immediate and eternal results, is obtained by the appropriation of the message of the gospel, which affirms the perdition of man because of his transgression of the laws of God; the necessity of a change of heart (Acts 2:38) and direction; and the identification of the sinner with Christ, the Son of God, Who came to give His life a ransom for many (Mark 10:45). The New Testament teaches us clearly that it is by the atoning death of Christ that men can be saved by being purified of their sins by the blood of the everlasting covenant (Mat. 26:28; Rom. 3:25, 26; Eph. 1:7; Col. 1:20; Heb. 9:12, 14, 26; 13:20; 1 Pet. 1:18, 19; 1 John 1:7; Rev. 5:9). No good work, no human act can deserve divine favour. The evangelical demand is clear: *"Ye must be born again"* (John 3:7).

Non-hereditary religion

That means that 1st century Christianity addresses directly the conscious individual and knows nothing of being assimilated to a hereditary religion, forms of paganism, Judaism, Islam or the major part of today's Christianity where men become at birth what their parents are. The apostolic churches were then churches of believers in which entry was by a personal spiritual experience, followed almost instantly by baptism.

Significance of baptism

It is in this context that we must place baptism, which could in no case be taken as a meritorious act, nor as a ceremony imposed on irrational individuals or as a means of salvation. Nevertheless, baptism is formally required and commanded by Christ (Mat. 28:19). It concerns all those who receive the gospel (Acts 2:41). It is an act of obedience to the Master, a visible sign or symbol of the invisible spiritual reality of the new birth, an act of witness and commitment, as well as a condition of entrance into the local church. Baptism is one of the distinctive marks of the disciple who wants to submit to the authority of his Master and follow His example. Christ, Himself, was baptized by John's baptism of repentance, not because He Himself had sinned, but because He identified Himself with sinful humanity (Mat. 3:13-16).

Baptism of the Spirit, experienced at the moment of the new birth, itself connected to the change of mind and to faith in Christ, preceded generally the baptism of water with which it was intimately linked to form an inseparable union to the point where Paul can speak of *"one baptism"* (Eph. 4:5).

The identification of the sinner with Christ in His death, in His burial and in His resurrection was best symbolized by an immersion, or rather a submersion, followed by an emergence (Rom.6:4, 5). Furthermore, the verb *"baptizein"* in Greek means to plunge, immerse, and the expressions used in the New Testament have this meaning: John *"baptized in Aenon near to Salim, because there was much water there"* (John 3:23); the notable Ethiopian and Philip *"went down both into the water"* and *"came up out of the water"* (Acts 8: 38).

The urgency of water baptism after conversion is expressed by Ananias to Paul: *"Why tarriest thou? arise, and be baptized…"* (Acts 22:16) and in Luke's account of Philippi's prison event *"... at the same hour of the night, and washed their stripes and was baptized..."* (Acts 16:33). The practice of certain churches today that have introduced a waiting period more or less long between conversion and water baptism may be a measure of wisdom, but it is entirely foreign to the New Testament.

Simplicity and spontaneity of Baptism

It is interesting to notice that there are no archaeological remains relating to baptism during the first century. Apart from the Jordan (Mat. 3:6) and Aenon, near to Salim (John 3:23), which are explicitly identified as places of baptism, we have no traces.

The baptisms took place in the open-air (rivers, ponds or sea) (Acts 8:36) or in ordinary buildings, without particular baptismal designation. Without doubt the pools of Jerusalem were used for numerous baptisms at Pentecost and perhaps the bath installations in the houses of Cornelius and of the jailor of Philippi or even in the basins in the atrium of ancient houses.

If there are no traces of buildings specially designated for baptism, neither are there traces of special baptismal liturgy. We can deduct from biblical records that one may have asked questions of the neophytes (Acts 8:37). Besides, we are certain that baptism itself was performed in the name of Jesus Christ (Acts 2:38), in the name of the Lord (Acts 19:5) or of the Trinity (Mat. 28:19), without being able to define more exactly the baptismal formula. Equally, there is no trace in the first century of any procedure for preparing for baptism or consecutive ceremonies to the act of baptism.

As to the one officiating at baptism, it was certainly the apostles that were baptizing (John 4:2), but we know that they were not the only ones to do it. We have at least two cases where it was deacon Philip (Acts 8:12, 13, 38, the Samaritans and the Ethiopian officer). There is also the case of Paul whom Ananias, a pious man, laid on hands before being baptized, probably by the same Ananias (Acts 9:17, 18). We equally know that Paul did not baptize all the Corinthians. They were no doubt baptized by one of Paul's co-labourers, Silas or Timothy (1 Cor. 1:13-16, Acts 18:5).

What we should like to stress, also, is that baptism was not a question of priesthood, nor of sacrament, in the first century. The terms *episcopoi* (bishops), *presbyteroi* (elders), *poimen* (shepherds or pastors) or *hegoumenoi* (leaders) applied to the same person. These terms are used interchangeably (Acts 20:17, 28; Titus 1:5, 7), and often in the plural, which signifies that there were several *episcopoi* or *presbyteroi* in the same church (cf. Philippi and Ephesus – Phil. 1:1 – Acts 11:30; 15:22 – Acts 20:17)[5]. We have to put forth a real effort to get rid of our traditional notions when we want to represent the churches of Jesus Christ in the first century, which were in principle congregationalist, autonomous, administered by a college of elders, and constituted exclusively of regenerated sinners, baptized by immersion (regenerate membership).

---

5   Léon X. Dufour, *Dictionary of N.T.*, Paris 1975 under "épiscope" and "presbytre".

2. THE PERIOD OF THE FIRST INNOVATIONS: SECOND AND THIRD CENTURIES

The second and third centuries brought modifications which prepared the way for more important changes during the following centuries.

Sprinkling

From the beginning of the second century, we ascertain that total immersion seems not to be considered as the only acceptable mode of baptism. Indeed, the *Didache*, an anonymous document, generally dated 120 A.D., gives precise instructions: "Concerning baptism, baptize in this way. Having first rehearsed all these things, baptize in the name of the Father and of the Son and of the Holy Ghost, in living water. But if you have not living water, baptize into other water; and, if thou canst not in cold, in warm. If you have neither, pour water thrice on the head in the name, etc. Before the baptism let the baptizer and the baptized fast, and others if they can. And order the baptized to fast one or two days before..."[6]

Is this a simple theoretic tolerance or is it the reflection of a rite already practised? We cannot say, but in any case, it can only be an exception, because total immersion is always preferred and will continue to be practised during long centuries. Affusion, will not be generally practised until after the paleochristian period.

The sacrament

It is towards the end of the second century that formulas appear among Christian authors tending to identify the sym-

---

[6]   *Didache* VII.

ool and the thing signified, that is to say, on the one hand water baptism, and on the other, the new birth, linked at its origin, as we have set forth, to repentance and to faith (Justin of Rome, Hermas, Irenaeus)[7]. This identification is progressively reinforced in the third century with Tertullian, whose theories on the baptismal water are already suspect[8], but who still strongly insists on the role of faith. One can even have the impression that Tertullian contradicts himself. On the one hand, he holds to the roots of the New Testament which teaches the necessity of faith[9], and on the other hand he tends toward the necessity of baptism for salvation and thus prepares the sacrament notion. That is why, while accepting infant baptism, he protests, around the year 200, against the lowering of the age of those baptized.

Against this, Cyprian, hardly fifty years later recommends the baptism of infants, born of Christian parents or not[10], immediately after their birth. The sacramental notion is defined and established. Parallel to the sacramental conception of baptism, here developed, of necessity, the doctrine of the priesthood, for in order to accomplish a quasi-magical act, you need an office with supernatural power, the priest. Cyprian also approved the practice of baptism for the bedridden by a simple affusion (clinical baptism). At the same time, the administration of the church evolved from the collegiality of the elders towards the unique episcopate of which the jurisdiction will spread beyond the local church to the combined metropolitan churches, and, finally to a whole region (diocese).

Justin of Rome, 1 *Apology,* 61 and 65; Hermas, *Similitudes* IX, 16 and 17. Irenaeus, *Against Heresies* III, 17.2.

Tertullian, *On Baptism* IV, 4, VI 1.

Tertullian, *On Baptism* XVIII, 5.

Cyprian, *Letters to Bishop Fidus.*

The house of the Christians of Doura Europos

As far as archaeology is concerned, a discovery of exceptional interest was made in 1931-32 at Doura Europos[11], on the banks of the Euphrates: a house built in the first century and used as a Christian meeting place in the first half of the third century, was discovered[12]. In spite of the fact that the house of the Christians of Doura Europos was the only one discovered of its kind, we can reasonably suppose that a number of similar places existed in the Roman Empire since the days of the apostles, where the Christians met in private houses of well-to-do faithful members of the church (Acts 2:46, 16:15; Rom. 16:5) until the end of the persecutions at the beginning of the fourth century.

Concerning this house of the Christians, a few remarks are in order:

a. There existed less than a century and a half after the disappearance of the last of the apostles, buildings reserved for Christian worship, even though they had not been built for that purpose. They had no particular architectural character. In his rescript of 313, Constantine orders that places of worship and belongings of the Christians, which were confiscated at the time of the persecutions, be restored to them. We have here an indication that permits us to think that the house of Doura Europos was not an isolated case.

b. At the beginning of the third century the baptismal room was already dissociated from the meeting room. No one was to enter the place of worship without having been baptized. Christian texts also confirm this practice. Later, the candidates for baptism (catechumens) were present for

---

[11] See also the comment on inside front cover.
[12] A. Grabar, *Le Premier Art Chrétien*, Paris, 1966, pp. 59-63, 67-71.

the celebration of the Lord's Supper in the narthex[13] of the churches. We discern here the beginnings of the construction of baptisteries independent of the sanctuaries, so widespread from the middle of the fourth century.

c. Great importance was put upon baptism. This is evident by the rich decoration of the walls and ceiling of the baptismal room, whereas the meeting room was simply whitewashed.

d. The candidates for baptism had to be adult believers, and baptism had to be administered by immersion in keeping with the dimensions of the baptismal pool. Christian texts of the third, fourth and even fifth centuries also amply confirm these requirements.

The persecutions of the second and third centuries compelled the Christians to remain more or less in the shadows in order not to draw the attention of the public authorities to their meetings. Perhaps it was one of the reasons for their using private houses: they were less identifiable and because of that fact, less vulnerable than the buildings of a specifically religious character.

---

[13] Portico.

3. THE PERIOD OF THE RADICAL TRANSFORMATION OF CHRISTIANITY: THE FOURTH CENTURY

Christianity becomes a lawful religion

With the fourth century, the modifications established in the second and third centuries are defined and emphasized, all the more since during the fourth century the attitude of the emperors toward Christianity was radically changed. Still persecuted by Diocletian and Galerius at the very beginning of the century, the Christians soon benefited from an edict of toleration signed by Galerius in 311 which ordered: *"The Christians are to pray to their God for our salvation, that of the empire and their own, in order that the integrity of the State be re-established everywhere, and that they will be able to live a peaceful life in their homes"*[14]. Christianity became a lawful religion. Thus a new stage is reached; two years later, the rescript of Milan (313), signed by Constantine and Licinius, put Christianity on an equal footing with paganism and gave instructions for procedures for restitution to the Christians of their places of worship and of their confiscated belongings[15].

Christianity becomes the official religion of the empire

During the reigns of Constantine and his successors (with the exception of the short pagan reaction of Julian the Apostate[16] (361-363), the favour of the emperors towards Christianity does not cease to increase up to the time that Theodosius prohibits paganism in Rome and in Alexandria in 391, and in the

---

[14] C. Lepelley, *L'Empire Romain et le Christianisme*, 1969, pp. 101, 102.
[15] Ibid, 1969, pp. 102, 103.
[16] More commonly called today "Julian the Philosopher"!

whole empire in 392. Christianity had become the official religion of the empire. All the subjects, young or old, were introduced, whether they liked it or not, into the church by baptism, generally without previous conversion and without personal conviction[17]. From then on, the nature of Christianity is fundamentally transformed. It became a hereditary, sacramental religion which was called *"Constantinian Christianity"* or *"Caesaro papism"*.

Appearance of basilicas and baptisteries

With the benediction and aid of the civil authorities, Christian basilicas appear in large numbers, as well as buildings exclusively designated for baptismal ceremonies. These baptisteries are constructed according to existing architectural models like thermal baths, fountains, mausoleums, etc., most often with a central plan[18].

If the archaeological discoveries of Christian remains of the second and third centuries are very scarce, they become more numerous especially from the second half of the fourth century onwards and even more so at the end of the century.

Thanks to excavations undertaken on the occasion of the restoration of ancient sanctuaries[19] and the intensification of archaeological research in general, baptismal installations were brought to light which permit us to arrive at a certain number of conclusions:

---

[17] F. Lot, *La Gaule*, Fayard 1967, p. 338 quote "Le christianisme a été... vie intérieure".

[18] A. Khatchatrian, *Origine et Typologie des Baptistères Paléochrétiens*, Mulhouse, 1982, pp. 7-15.

[19] Cathedral St Pierre at Genève, Church St Etienne beside the Cathedral St Jean at Lyon, Cathedral at Aoste, Cathedral of Reims.

a. baptismal pools, generally octagonal in the west and cruciform in the east, are established in **special buildings,** which signifies that baptism was still a condition for entrance into the church;

b. the baptisteries are decorated with marble (in the richest communities) or symbolic subjects in mosaics, which underlines **the importance** attached to the act of baptism;

c. the **dimension** of baptismal pools permits us to conclude the practice of total immersion of adults. For example, the pool (cruciform) of Mariana (Corsica, fig. 5) was 2 m in diameter[20]; the one of Geneva (octagonal, fig. 11) was 2.50 m in diameter[21]; the one of Lyon (octagonal, fig. 2) was 3 m in diameter[22]; the one of Cazères (also octagonal, fig. 4) was 1.20 m in diameter and 1.13 m in depth[23];

d. it is significant to notice that at a later period, during the fifth or sixth century, these same pools were reduced once or twice in surface or in depth, so that in their final phase the pools of Mariana (fig. 5), of Geneva (fig. 11) and of Lyon (fig. 2) had only 0.70-0.76 m, and 1.20 and 1.95 m in diameter respectively, and the one of Cazères (fig. 4) had only 0.48 m in depth.

One could add those of Köln and Reims, as well as a certain number of cases in other parts of the

[20] Mariana: Mazel G. Moracchini, *Les monuments paléochrétiens de la Corse*, Paris, 1967, pp. 7-78

[21] Genève: C. Bonnet, *Archéologie Suisse*, 1980, pp. 174-191.

[22] Lyon: J.F. Raynaud, *Le groupe épiscopal de Lyon*, Paris, 1976.

[23] Cazères: G. Manière, *Le site antique de Bantayré. Mémoire de la Société d'Architecture du Midi de la France*, 1972.

Mediterranean area or of the North of the Alps: Aoste, Riva San Vitale, Saint Maurice d'Agaune, Zurzach.

It is evident that these examples, chosen among others, indicate a change in the liturgy and a transition from total immersion of an adult to partial immersion, by different affusions of an adult to the total or partial immersion of children, to end up with the sole affusion of infants. Although this evolution cannot be rigorously established in all cases or in all regions at the same period, it is beyond question that we observe an evolution that generally goes in that direction[24].

The Christian written documents of this period confirm the practice of a triple immersion conferred on adults having followed serious instruction for several weeks (Cyril of Jerusalem, at the middle of the fourth century[25] [see appendix VII] and Theodor of Mopsueste at the end of the fourth century[26]).

The meaning of baptism, having already evolved from symbol to sacrament in the second and third centuries, further evolved from a rite to blot out all sin at the beginning of the fourth century (from whence the delayed baptisms of a certain number of known persons, among them Gregory of Nazianze, Basil the Great, Chrysostom, Jerome, even the emperor Constantine), towards a sacrament to blot out original sin, especially after the formulation of the doctrine by Augustine (from whence precocious baptisms of newborn babes practised in the Middle Ages until this day). Mgr. Duchèsne said

---

[24] F. Buhler, *Schéma de l'évolution du baptême et des installations baptismales*, Mulhouse, 1982.

[25] Cyrille de Jérusalem, *Cathéchèses Mystagogiques*, II,4.

[26] Théodore de Mopsueste, *Les homélies catéchétiques, 3ᵉ homélie sur le baptême*, 18,19.

that in the fourth century one went "from the baptistery to the grave". After Augustine to the contrary, one could say that one went from the cradle to the baptistery, nevertheless not in an absolute manner, for the baptism of children was not generalized by the seventh or eighth centuries in certain regions.

4. THE PERIOD WHEN THE CHANGES ARE DEFINED AND CONSOLIDATED: BEGINNING IN THE FIFTH CENTURY

The Christian archaeological testimonies are more and more numerous. They confirm the idea already put forward that the evolution is not everywhere uniform. In certain regions baptismal pools are still rather large to permit the immersion of an adult and in others are already too small to practise such an immersion in them. Observation confirms the shrinking of certain pools already smaller in their first stage than those of the fourth century (Zurzach, fig. 10; Riva san Vitale, fig. 9; Saint-Maurice d'Agaune fig. 8)[27]. Several pools of the sixth and seventh centuries discovered in Nubia, notably at Dongolo[28], also show a shrinking, which proves that the evolution in question is not limited to Europe.

The chief of the Holy Roman Empire, Emperor Charlemagne, new Constantine, but less tolerant than the first, decreed in the ordinance of the Saxons (785) the death penalty for all violations of "Christian principles", among which, the refusal of baptism for oneself or for one's children. These instructions were not left as dead letters, since several thousand Saxons were massacred for that reason. One could hardly go further in contempt of biblical conditions for baptism! In making baptism a civic duty, Charlemagne went all the way to the ultimate consequence of "caesaro-papism". At that period, baptism was still practised by immersion and even by triple immersion, which arises from a tract of Magnus, bishop of Sens, written under the order of this same Charlemagne.

---

[27] Zurzach: Lauert-Belart, *Eine Frühchristliche Kirche in Zurzach*, in Ur-Schweitz 4, 1955.
Riva S. Vitale: D. Seste, *Il battistero di Riva San Vitale*, Bellinzona, 1947.
Saint-Maurice: L. Blondel, *Le Baptistère et les Anciens Edifices Conventuels de l'Abbaye d'Agaune dans Vallesia*, 1949, pp. 15-28.
[28] W. Faras Godlewski VI, *Les Baptistères Nubiens*, Varsovie 1979, pp. 98-115.

Progressively, pools are replaced by **baptismal fonts**, and the baptisteries, as independent buildings, disappear in France in the eleventh century. The baptisms of children are celebrated in baptismal chapels inside the churches. In contrast, in Italy, one observes the late construction of baptisteries from the pre-Roman period up until the Gothic period.

The famous baptisteries of Florence, Pisa, Parma Varese, Volterra, Lenno, Vintimille, Albenga, among many others, are of this period and often shelter pools where an adult immersion is still possible. Even later, St. Charles Borromée, who presided at the Council of Milan (1576), ordered the restoration of existing baptisteries and the building of new ones.

Codification of the changes

It is in the course of this period and following the twelfth century (Lateran Council) that the most important dogmas of the catholic church were defined. A little later the Council of Trent (1545-1563) finally codified that which was vague and in evolution during long centuries. In its 14 canons adopted during the seventh session (March 3, 1547) it confirmed the nature of baptism, its significance and its place among the other sacraments in defining that:

- baptism is really a sacrament, that is to say *"an efficacious sign of the grace it produces";*
- baptism is one of the seven sacraments, with confirmation, eucharist, penance, extreme unction, holy orders and matrimony;
- baptism in blotting out original sin is *"necessary for salvation";*
- baptism imprints a *"character"* (an indelible spiritual mark) like confirmation and holy orders.[29]

---

[29] *Histoire des Conciles*, Tome X, *Les Décrets du Concile de Trente*, Paris, 1938, pp. 198, 199, 201, 208.

With these canons we are very far removed from the immersion symbol conferred on only repentant sinners during the apostolic period.

In the twentieth century

As for our own age it is worthwhile to point out certain nostalgia for the ancient models.

In several cities after the Second World War, churches were built with a baptistery more or less separate from the sanctuary and which, in addition, recalls the ancient pools by the steps which go down to the baptismal fonts. Even for the mode of baptism, one notices an inclination to return to the primitive model. In the recent "Baptismal ritual for children of school age" (1977), approved by the Commission for the sacraments and divine worship, it is suggested:

"To give more fullness to the sign, as is desirable, one can confer baptism by total immersion, or in plunging under water the head of the child" (cf. the Ambrosian rite practised in the province of Milan). But that wish has not yet been realized, according to the enquiry which we made among competent persons. Furthermore, the orthodox church continues to practise triple immersion of infants.

But we are still far removed, alas, from biblical baptism which required the experience of conversion, that is to say, the engagement of a good conscience and a spiritual identification with Christ in His death and in His resurrection (Rom. 6).

CONCLUSIONS OF THE FIRST SECTION

The study of baptismal installations discovered by the archaeologists and the parallel study of texts on baptism, beginning with the New Testament, bring to mind a series of reflections on the evolution of the practice and meaning of baptism.

The episcopal problem

It was believed for a very long time that baptism was in the paleo-christian period, an episcopal prerogative. It was stated that the baptismal installations were found only in cities where a bishop resided. The discovery of several baptismal installations in the same city (Rome, Naples, Milan) as well as the discovery of baptismal pools in localities which, from all evidence, were not the seat of a bishop, like the fortlet of the danubian and rhenan Limes, led the archaeologists and the historians to abandon that notion of episcopal prerogative *"at least for the later periods"* (cf. Mrs. Nicolajevic of Belgrade, M. Noël Duval of Paris, Mr. P.-A. Fevrier of Aix)[30].

In our first part, we stated the fact that the New Testament speaks of bishops and presbyters interchangeably, and generally in the plural, when it concerns the same church. In the neotestamentary period, and even a long time after, all the churches were "Episcopalian"! One can thus ask oneself if the misunderstanding does not have its origin, in part at least, in the ambiguity of the term bishop employed today in the sense of the head of a diocese, whereas at the beginning and during a rather extended period the term did only designate ordinary, responsible leaders of a local community[31].

---

[30] F. Buhler, *Occupation Romaine des Régions Rhénanes et Questions Posées par les Installations Baptismales des Ouvrages Militaires*, Mulhouse, 1984, p. 21.

[31] Léon Dufour X, *Dictionnaire du N. T.* , Paris, 1975, sous "épiscope" et "presbytre".

The testimony of iconography

Christian iconography permits us equally to follow the stages of the evolution of baptismal liturgy.

Up until the twelfth century approximately, in the numerous representations of His baptism, Christ is in the water up to his hips[32], or up to the waist[33], or even up to the neck[34] (fig. 14). It can only refer to baptism by total or almost total immersion. John the Baptist stretches out his right hand towards Christ's head and holds in his left hand a roll or codex[35].

From the thirteenth century, Christ is represented with water up to the knees[36], up to half-calf[37] or even only up to the ankles[38]. John is then represented pouring water on the head of Jesus often by means of a scallop shell (fig. 15)[39].

The mode of baptism

In another connection, we are struck, we who are used to baptismal fonts in which the newborn are "baptized": by the dimensions of baptismal pools of the fourth century discovered during these last decades in different countries of the West and to the North of the Alps.

The last period of the pools mentioned allowed a newborn to

---

[32] Giotto, 1266-1336, *Chapelle des Scrovegni*, Padoue.

[33] Florence: Baptistère San Giovanni, 12th century.

[34] *Chapiteau historié*, Musée d'Unterlinden, Colmar. Provenance: monastery St. Marc, 1130, as well as Mosaïque of the monastery St. Luc of Phocide, about 1000.

[35] = book.

[36] Liber Chronicorum, 1493.

[37] Monastery Unterlinden, Peinture end of XVIth century.

[38] Verrochio, 1436-1488.

[39] Fresque sous porche du baptistère de Baveno (Lac Majeur), after XVIth century.

be "baptized" by immersion, a practice witnessed in the Middle Ages and at the time of the Reformation. We, however, established that the first traces of a possibility of affusion is already uncovered in the *Didache* (beginning of the 2nd century) and the baptism of children was practised from the end of the second century, or at the beginning of the third century, at least in North Africa. But these practices, which are already deviations from the apostolic era, are not prescribed in certain regions before the seventh century, and in certain others a few centuries later.

A real desire to come back to the sources is evident today. Persons affiliated with churches traditionally paedo-baptist are being immersed and we cited the instructions of the recent "Ritual of Baptism for children of school age". This nostalgia for immersion corresponds, perhaps, to the renewal of Scriptural studies, and to a better understanding of the biblical significance of immersion, perfect symbol of death, burial with Christ and the resurrection to newness of life in Him.

Baptism of children

The scantiness of baptismal pools of the fifth to the seventh centuries amply proves that at a certain period the total immersion of adults was abandoned. These pools could be used for partial immersion of adults with water affusion or for the baptism of children, either by total or partial immersion, or by simple affusion. Lucas Cranach portrayed a child baptism at the time of the Reformation. The officiating person holds the child still dripping with water over a fairly large baptismal pool. At the same epoch, Luther explains that "Taufe" = baptism, came from "tief" = deep, which implies an immersion.

Concerning the baptism of children, we know that at the end of the second century, Tertullian was opposed to the baptism of little children whereas Cyprian, toward the middle of the third century was an ardent defender of the baptism of children, even newborns. A text of Hippolyte of Rome of the first half of the third century[40] foresees in the course of the same baptismal ceremony, first, the baptism of children, conscious or not, followed by that of adult men and, to conclude, that of women, which proves that different modes of baptism were practised simultaneously.

It seems, furthermore, that the baptism of children had its origin in North Africa, country of Tertullian and Cyprian, and that it was finally adopted in Spain during the sixth century and in other countries only in the sixteenth century.

The significance of baptism
A more important question than the mode of baptism is the significance of baptism. When the spiritual experience was no longer required as a condition for baptism, especially from the fourth century when all the subjects of the empire, without distinction, were introduced into the church, baptism was supposed to **accomplish** that which it previously **symbolized,** and one attributed to baptism the virtue of blotting out sins, and more particularly, original sin.

By reason of the evolution of theology, one thus came to baptismal regeneration, still in practice today in the Roman Catholic Church. The Reformers of the sixteenth century, while rejecting baptismal regeneration and in proclaiming salvation by grace, through faith, neverthe-

---

[40] Hippolyte de Rome, *Tradition Apostolique. Le Baptême et l'Eucharistie.*

less, maintained the baptism of little children as a sign of the covenant of grace by replacing circumcision, sign of the old covenant.

All is linked together

In thinking over the archaeological discoveries, one may well understand how things depend on each other. If baptism is a **sacrament**, that is a supernatural act, priesthood is imperative. It must have, in principle, a priest with supernatural powers to administer it (except for cases of emergency where a lay person can intervene). As the sacrament operates by itself, it is not necessary for the subject to be able to reason, newborns can benefit from it. Baptismal installations then can be reduced as well as immersion, and instead be linked to the symbolic conception of baptism, and thus an anachronism. It is sufficient that the water run on the forehead of the baby. In that case, baptismal fonts containing little water were perfectly suitable.

If, on the other hand, baptism is a **symbol** of death and resurrection with Christ, it goes without saying that only adult subjects, youths or even children, able to reason, having experienced repentance and faith in Christ can be valid candidates. Total immersion is then the most eloquent image of this burial in the symbolic tomb, which necessitated baptismal installations of a certain dimension, as the pools we have mentioned[41].

Archaeology is thus the revealer of the evolution of the dogma and the baptismal practice. On the one hand we easily understand:

---

[41] F. Buhler, *Tableau de l'évolution du baptême au cours des siècles*, Mulhouse, 1985.

- the progressive shrinking of the surface and depth of the baptismal pools;

- the substitution of the sacrament for the symbol;

- the substitution of the unknowing infant for the repentant sinner.

On the other hand we equally understand that face to face with what has unfortunately become a caricature of truly biblical Christianity established by Christ and the apostles, certain Christians are really anxious to follow their Master's desire to return to the biblical models:

- the immersion of repentant sinners;

- that which follows logically, a professing church.

In the second section of this book, we will see the exclusive biblical aspects further developed than on pages 12 and 13. It will be a return to the sources.

SECOND SECTION

BIBLICAL ASPECTS OF BAPTISM, RETURN TO THE SOURCES

BIBLICAL ASPECTS OF BAPTISM,
RETURN TO THE SOURCES

Having arrived at the end of the archaeological and historical section of our study, we cannot help but ask ourselves the meaning of this evolution over the centuries.

It clearly appears to us that the practice of baptism is now very different from what it was originally.

The question which we can and must ask is in relation to baptism as it is generally practised today in the mainline churches:

- are we in the presence of a happy evolution which is going towards an ideal to be attained, or

- are we in the presence of a regrettable evolution characterized by the abandonment of the model originally established?

In the first case, one could wish that, thanks to a continued development, to new revelations and to new dogmas, we will reach, in a more or less distant future, the final goal still unknown today. We know well from whence we have come, but we do not know where we are going.

In the second case, we evidently know also from whence we have come, but our supreme ambition should be to return to that source which we should never have abandoned.

Several reasons make us decide for this second position, even though it may appear more static than dynamic. To our understanding it is intimately linked to the divine immutability (Heb 13:8, James 1:17).

1. GENERAL OBSERVATIONS

a. In the Holy Scriptures, we have innumerable exhortations to return to God and His law. The general tendency of the Jews and later the Christians was to wander from God and His revelation. In the beginning, *"God saw all that He had made, and behold, it was very good"* (Gen. 1:31), but two chapters further on we already read the account of the Fall (Gen. 3:1-16) and soon after the text says: *"And God saw that the wickedness of man was great in the earth, and that every imagination of the thoughts of his heart was only evil continually"* (Gen. 6:5). The first sin consisted, in fact, to live independently of God and His commandment. That wretched experience, so fraught with unfortunate consequences for all men, was constantly renewed in the course of the history of humanity.

One could recall, in this connection, the second law of thermo-dynamics which states that every isolated system, left to itself, loses progressively its energy, degenerates, and experiences disorder (entropy). In the same manner Christianity on the whole, as well as the "Christian" individual, who does not stay in direct and constant intimacy with God, source of all true spiritual energy, falls, degenerates and sinks into chaos. The Christian and the work of God have to do with a subtle enemy, Satan, whose supreme object is to hinder or prevent the development desired by God, by bringing men to ruin by making them deviate from the way traced by God.

These deviations, caused by false prophets were, furthermore, expressly announced by Jesus Himself (Mat. 24:11) by His apostles: Peter (2 Pet. 2:1, 2), Paul (Acts 20:30, 1 Tim. 4:1-3), John (1 John 4:1-6) and by Jude (v.4).

b. Christ and His apostles bequeathed us a perfect Christianity, issuing from a progressive revelation throughout the previous centuries. Furthermore, Christ is the last word of God, the most perfect messenger of the divine revelation (Heb. 1:1, 2). In fact, He is the Word incarnate (John 1:14). So to the apostles, Christ promised the help of the Holy Spirit to lead them into all truth (John 14:26; 16:13). This implies that at the moment of their disappearance, all that they could and should know to communicate and transmit truth to others had been revealed to them. At the very end of the first century, John is still beneficiary of this promise, but his ministry marks the end of the promised revelation. That is where the biblical canon comes to its conclusion. We do not possess one single divinely inspired book subsequent to the twenty-seven books, which make up our New Testament. Christianity, from its origins, is not susceptible to amelioration. All ulterior changes could only be deviations.

c. The Scriptures themselves underscore the necessity to stay true to the Gospel as it was proclaimed at the beginning. The Christians of Jerusalem understood it very well. They continued in the doctrine of the apostles (Acts 2:42). That was one of the four characteristics of that church, the other three being fellowship, the breaking of bread and prayers. Paul affirms that the Gospel which he communicated to the Corinthians guarantees salvation on condition that they hold it as he had announced it to them (1 Cor. 15:1, 2). The perseverance in maintaining the doctrine of the apostles is, in fact, the true "apostolic succession".

d. In seeing with surprise and sorrow the rapid abandonment of the Gospel by the Galatians (Gal 1:6), Paul affirms the necessity to refuse all gospels other than

that which they had received from him. He was so convinced that in no way was that Gospel to be modified, that he pronounced anathema upon any who would announce another Gospel, even if it were he or an angel from heaven (Gal. 1:8, 9). The apostle energetically struggled for the maintenance of the integrity of the Gospel toward and against all (Gal. 2:5).

e. **John writes at the end of the *"Revelation of Jesus Christ[42]"* that curses attend those who permit themselves to add anything to his book or who would take away anything** (Rev. 22:19). From all evidence, he has in mind the book which he has just written, but in considering that which precedes, it is right and logical to apply this stricture also to the whole of the sacred text.

All that teaches us that the Christianity of the end of the first century is binding and, because of this, it is not only wise and expedient but essential to maintain it and come back to it, if we really want to conform to the plan of God. Many have understood this principle. During the centuries there were many attempts to return to the sources. They did not all succeed. Even the Reformation of the sixteenth century with its excellent motto *"Sola Scriptura"* did not succeed because of holding onto infant baptism and the hereditary character of *"faith"*. As one became catholic through birth into a catholic family, one also became a protestant by birth into a protestant family.

f. **According to the Scripture, it is not by birth that one becomes a Christian, but by the new birth.** An eminent servant of God of the first centuries affirmed it in saying. *"One is not born a Christian, but becomes one!"*[43] ***"That***

---

[42] Or Apocalypse.

[43] Tertullian, *Apologetic*, XVIII, 4.

which is born of the flesh is flesh and that which is born of the Spirit is spirit" (John 3:6).

In the same manner that we have written several chapters on the deviations of the church and of baptism in the course of the centuries in the first section of this study, we could write several chapters on the reconquest of the primitive Christian ideal and in particular of baptism. However, we will restrict ourselves to recall the varied aspects of apostolic baptism to do honour to the texts of the New Testament.

2. THE CHARACTERISTICS OF SCRIPTURAL BAPTISM

a. Baptism is first of all an act of obedience to Christ. It is the first step of the disciple on the road of submission to his Master. The disciple is, by definition, the person who receives the Lord into his life, who welcomes His teaching and who follows His example. He is more than a simple student who would be content to attend the courses of a teacher without changing his behaviour. On the contrary, he attaches himself to his Master and Lord and adopts His mode of thinking and life.

The command of Christ indicates the steps to follow: *"Go, make disciples of all nations, baptize them... and teach them to observe all things I have commanded you."* (Mat. 28:19). The exhortation of Peter on the day of Pentecost confirms the same command: *"Repent and be baptized everyone of you..."*. By repentance one acknowledges the error of his ways for the receiving of pardon and undertakes to change his ways. *"Those who received his word were baptized"* (Acts 2:38, 41). Baptism was the test of obedience. *"He who believes and is baptized shall be saved"* (Mark 16:16). That baptism is neither a condition nor a means of salvation is brought out by the fact that Jesus adds: *"He that believeth not shall be damned"* (Mark 16:16). In the same way, the assurance Jesus gives to the thief on the cross proves that baptism is not necessary to salvation (Luke 23:43) and similarly with the presence of believers of the old covenant in glory (Heb. 11:39, 40; 12:23). Neither one nor the others were baptized. They nevertheless benefited from "eternal" glory, "because they are saved by grace (*sola gratia*) through faith (*sola fide*)" according to Ephesians 2:8.

One must not, however, conclude that baptism is secondary or optional. Baptism is an integral part of the apostolic message (Acts 2:38). All those who believed were baptized (Acts 2:41;

8:12; 9:18; 10:47, 48; 16:15, 33; 18:8, etc.), with the exception of those mentioned above to which baptism was an impossibility. Submission to the command of Christ (Mat. 28:19) and the imitation of His example (Luke 3:21) are binding upon the disciple worthy of His name.

Even the urgency of baptism is seen in the case of Paul: *"Why tarriest thou, arise and be baptized"* (Acts 22:16) and that of the jailer: *"At that same hour of the night... at once he was baptized..."* (Acts 16:33).

Baptism must not be put off unduly after conversion.

One can be saved without baptism, but one cannot be a real "Christian", that is to say a disciple of Christ (Acts 11:26) without baptism and, further, not any kind of baptism, but the immersion of the believer. All other modes of baptism are not biblical.

b. Biblical baptism is also the visible sign of an invisible spiritual reality but manifested by its effects. The New Testament presents us with several water baptisms:

1. the baptism of John was a baptism unto repentance (Luke 3:3; Acts 19:4).

2. the baptism practised by Christ and the apostles was, further, a baptism of identification with Jesus as Lord (John 4:1, 2).

3. the baptism practised after Pentecost is the true Christian baptism. It expresses in a symbolic way the identification of the new convert with Christ in His death and in His resurrection (Rom. 6:4-6). The experience of the new birth (John 3:3), the birth of the Spirit (John 3:6) or the baptism of the Spirit (Acts 1:5), preceded by the experience of death unto self (Luke 9:23) and to sin (Rom. 6:2) is illustrated by a burial under water (immersion or rather sub-

mersion) and an emersion out of the water like coming out of a tomb. The immersion and consecutive emersion constitute, without any doubt, the most expressive image of a death followed by a spiritual resurrection (Eph. 2:4-6).

In the apostolic period, the water could be any kind of water: *"Here is water, what hinders me to be baptized?"* (Acts 8:36), and the act was not a sacrament, as Philip was not a priest. Nothing happened that could give the impression of grace received by baptism. Such an act did not necessitate, at that time, special virtue on the part of the baptizer. The priesthood did not occur before the end of the second century at the time when the sacrament came to be. At the origin it was not water that blotted out sin, but rather the blood of Christ, lamb without fault or blemish. This is strongly confirmed by the following texts taken among others: Mat. 26:28; Rom. 3:25, 26; Eph. 1:7; Col. 1:20; Heb. 9:12, 14, 26; 13:20; 1 Pet. 1:18, 19; 1 John 1:7; Rev. 5:9.

As baptism is a symbol of a spiritual experience, it can only have its true significance in the case of persons having passed through conversion, which excludes unknowing infants and unregenerated adults.

c. Baptism is then a testimony and a commitment. The newly converted who passes through the waters of baptism proclaims before his brothers and even the unconverted, the reality of his meeting with the Lord. He bears testimony that he has passed from death unto life, from darkness to light, from the slavery of Satan and sin to the liberty of the children of God. He then identifies himself with Christ his Saviour to whom he owes eternal life and his Master to whom he wants to consecrate his earthly life. As Christians by their participation in communion proclaim the Lord's death until He comes (1 Cor. 11:26), in the same way the individual believer proclaims, by his baptism, the death and resurrection of Christ as the foundation of salvation. That is why baptism is practised in the presence of witnesses, which witness the testimony given and the new status of the baptized. By being baptized, the believer justifies God by his submission to this ordinance, as the people and publicans did in the time of John the Baptist (Luke 7:29, 30).

By his obedience to the commands of Christ, the newly baptized testifies to his desire to live in newness of life (2 Cor. 5:17; Rom. 6:4). In recognizing Christ as his Saviour, he solemnly pledges himself to submit to Him for the remainder of his earthly pilgrimage. The commitment is unique, like baptism, but submission must be renewed day after day. The vain conversation received by tradition from your fathers (1 Pet. 1:18) should no longer have any attraction for the baptized. If he is still **in** the world, he is no longer **of** the world (John 17:11,14). The world is crucified unto him, as he is crucified unto the world (Gal. 6:14).

d. Finally, baptism is an enrolment. By baptism, the believer is not only united to Christ, but also to his brothers in the bosom of a local church. Those who were baptized on the day of Pentecost were added to the church of Jerusalem (Acts 2:41, 47). Paul, in speaking of the baptism of the Spirit, inseparable from water baptism with which he forms a union, says: *"we have, in fact, all been baptized into one spirit to form one body"* (1 Cor. 12:13; Rom. 12:5).

The process, begun at the moment of personal conversion, ends up logically in collective life. We are in the presence of a succession of invariable experiences which show that baptism cannot constitute an independent reality. In fact, it constitutes a link in a chain which must not be left out, neither displaced, in one sense or in another. The sequence of the facts takes off at the sending of the messenger, passes by the proclamation of the message, by its acceptance in repentance, and in faith, by submission to baptism. It continues by entrance into the church, the Christian life and service in the bosom of the church, producing the fruit of the Spirit (Gal. 5:22), exercising spiritual gifts (1 Cor. 12:7), and culminates in the "*unity of the faith and the knowledge of the Son of God*" (Eph. 4:13), resulting in "*a body fitly joined together and compacted*" (Eph. 4:16). This unity manifests itself more particularly in the Lord's Supper (1 Cor. 10:17). After having been an individual living in guilty independence before God and man, the Christian ends up being like his brothers, a member of the body of Christ.

Today we find a great confusion in relation to this divine program: persons are being "baptized" before being converted; others are converted without being baptized; others content themselves with a "baptism" which is not the immersion of the believer; still others, the most numerous, are members of an organization which is not a biblical church which, by definition, is made up of converted individuals, independent of the State and of every other external authority (cf. Appendix IV/Remarks).

We are invited not to ignore, nor forget, the significance of our baptism (Rom. 6:3), and not to be tempted to return to our old life style according to the world (Rom. 12:2, Titus 2:11, 12). It is in the fellowship with brothers and sisters that the new member strives to follow the instructions of the Head of the church which is His body (Eph. 1:22, 23), for his own welfare and that of all the other members (1 Cor. 12:7; 1 Pet. 4:10).

Baptism, even though it is not a sacrament, is not just an act void of any meaning or a simple formality. It is, to the contrary, fraught with significance. We have, in effect, been able to establish that it expresses the relationship of the believer:

• with his Saviour whom he wants to follow (act of obedience) and with whom he identifies (symbol of the death and spiritual resurrection);

- with men, in general, to whom he communicates his experience of salvation (testimony);

- with the children of God, in particular, with whom he associates to engage in service in the bosom of the church led by the Lord (commitment and enrolment).

GENERAL CONCLUSION

By going back to the source, all evolution, all the deviations arising in the course of the centuries in relation to the ideal of God presented in the New Testament are neutralized.

By returning to the source, we will accomplish the will of God, which consists in putting back in the place of honour the model of the local church in its different aspects.

The church is:

1. **An organism rather than an organization,** administered according to the congregational principle, separate from the State, independent of all external authority, led by an elder or a college of elders.

2. **A community constituted of converted sinners** by the working of the Spirit, immersed on profession of their faith, producing the fruit of the Spirit, exercising the gift or gifts which the Spirit bestows to each one for the building up of the believers and for the salvation of men in the world.

3. **A body in submission to the head**, which communicates its will by the Holy Scriptures rendered comprehensible by the action of the Holy Spirit and by the ministry of pastors-teachers (Eph. 4:11).

A return to the source will not be a step backward but, in reality, a step forward towards the goal prepared by God for all eternity: the union of Christ with His church which He loved, for which He gave Himself and which He purchased with the price of His sacrifice on the cross of Calvary (Eph. 5:25; Rev. 19:7). *"This glorious church, not having spot or wrinkle, or any such thing, but holy and without blemish"* will appear before Him and will contemplate the glory of the Lord for all eternity (Eph. 5:27; John 17:24).

"Now unto him that is able to do exceeding abundantly above all that we ask or think, according to the power that worketh in us, unto him, be glory in the church by Christ Jesus throughout all ages, world without end. Amen" (Eph. 3:20, 21).

ILLUSTRATIONS, PHOTOS, COMMENTARIES

Photo credits:

Fig. 1: The house of the Christians of Doura-Europos: Work of A. Grabar, *The First Christian Art*, Gallimard (with kind permission of Yale University Art Gallery)

Fig. 4: Section of the pool of Cazères, by M. Manière

Fig. 12: Pool of Martigny, by F. Wiblé or H.-J. Lehner

Other photos are by the author.

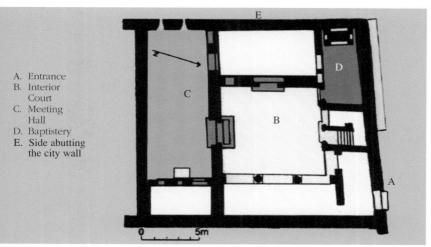

A. Entrance
B. Interior Court
C. Meeting Hall
D. Baptistery
E. Side abutting the city wall

Fig 1: Doura-Europos (Syria). The house of the Christians of the city. At left, meeting hall (C) dated 232 whitewashed. At right, baptistery (D) decorated with frescoes (E) side abutting the city wall – at present in the art gallery, Yale University (USA). Exterior dimensions of the pool, 1.25 x 2.50 m.

Fig. 2: Lyon (Rhône). Beside the "primatiale" St. Jean, archaeological park, remains of the St. Etienne church. Baptismal pool under plastic cover. Section of the wall of the pool which represents three stages of construction (initial diameter 3 m, final 1.95 m). At left, remains of the pool, still large in its final stage. The curved-in part is probably the place of the one officiating.

Fig. 3: Nice (Alpes Maritimes). Baptistery installed in the thermal baths of the city of Cemenelum (Cimiez). The large columns are elevated on the ancient bases. Pool relatively small, the one officiating could not be in the water with the candidate at baptism.

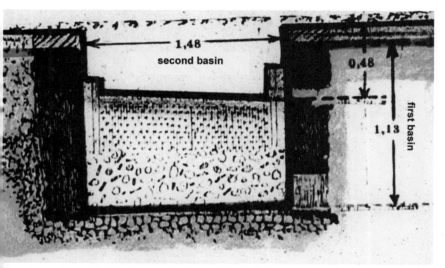

Fig. 4: Cazères (Haute Garonne). Two stages of construction: the first stage was 1.13 m deep and the second at 0.48 m. The only case known where the shrink-age was done vertically.

Fig. 5: Mariana (Haute Corse). The first pool is cruciform with diameter of 2 m. The second is octagonal, and the third, which is well seen, is circular with a diameter of 0.70 m to 0.76 m. The installation dates at the end of the 4th century or at the latest at the beginning of the 5th century.

Fig. 6: Corte (Haute Corse). Paleo-christian site with basilica and baptistery. One sees the apse of the church with the mural bands to the left and at the center the baptistery (trefoil building) separated from the church with a small baptismal pool. No doubt not the initial pool.

Fig. 7: Lioli (Haute Corse). Example of a pre-roman chapel which served religious, liturgical and judicial functions, after the paleo-christian period. The remains of other baptismal pools were found partially below ground level. Here the pool was reconstructed (front center).

Fig. 8: St. Maurice d'Agaune (Valais). In the cloister of the Abbey of Agaune, baptismal pool of 1.48 m to 1.56 m in diameter and depth of 0.65 m.

Fig. 9: Riva San Vitale (Tessin). Two superimposed pools: one octagonal underneath the ground level and a circular monolith above ground level (1.90 m in diameter).

Fig. 10: Zurzach (Argovie). In a roman fortress, remains of a paleo-christian church, baptismal installation originally 1.10 m square, reduced to 0.90 m x 0.50 m.

Fig 11:
Geneva. First baptismal pool discovered under the cathedral at Geneva. Initial diameter 2.50 m reduced to 1.20 m. Other older pools were found at lower levels.

Fig. 12: Martigny (Valais). Under the present parish church remains of the two Middle age churches and baptismal pool nearly quadrangular with dimensions 1.20 m x 0.90 m. The pool seems small for baptism by immersion.

Fig. 13: Glis, near Brigue (Valais). The original baptistery served as a burial place. The white remains indicate a baptismal pool big enough to receive the body of an adult (dimensions of the skeleton), thus total immersion in a shallow depth of water.

Fig. 14: Colmar (Ht. Rhin). Unterlinden Museum. Historiated capital representing Christ in the water up to the neck. Sculpture of the convent of St. Mark, 11th century.

Fig. 15:
Baveno, Lac Majeur (Italy). The fresco under the porch of the baptistery is the reproduction of the baptism of Christ with a minimum of water. Jesus does not even have his feet in the water. This reproduction is late (about 14th or 15th century).

Fig. 16:
Montpellier (Hérault). Archaeological Museum, capital of the Abbey of Psalmody. Jesus is represented seated in the water. The right hand of John is on the right shoulder of Christ, the left hand has disappeared. It was placed on the bosom of Christ (left side).

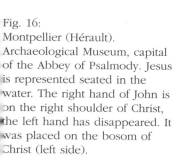

APPENDICES

Descriptions

APPENDIX I

The sudden important religious reversal: from the persecution to the recognition of Christianity by the Roman Emperors of the IVth century.

Emperors

West	East
Numerianus and Corinus 283	
Diocletian, sole emperor 284-305	
Division of the Empire: The Tetrarchy	
Maximian (Trèves, Milan) 285-305	Diocletian (Nicomedia) 284-305
Constantius Chlore (Trèves) 293-306	Galerius (Thessalonica) 293-311
Constantine (Gaul, Brittany) 306-312	
Maxence (Italy and Africa) 306-312	Licinius 308-324
Constantine, sole emperor 324-337	
Constantine II (Gaul) 337-340	Constans II 337-350
Constans (Italy) 337-350	
Constans II, sole emperor 351-361	
Julian the Apostate 361-363	
Jovian 363-364	
Valentinian I 364-375	Valens 364-378
Gratian 367-383	
Valentinian II 375-392	Theodosius 379-394
Theodosius, sole emperor 394-395	
Honorius 395-423	Arcadius 395-408

Bibliography: C. Lepelley, *The Roman Empire and Christianity Historical Questions* - Flammarion 1969.

Recalling of principal events marking the first centurie of the Christian era (bordering the question of baptism)

303 Four last edicts of persecution under Diocletian and Galerius

304 **Christianity is a forbidden religion: Christians are persecuted**

305 Abdication of Maximien and Diocletian

311 (April 30) - Edict of Toleration of Galerius (very ill; ask ing Christians to pray for his salvation, that of the Empire and for themselves). **Christianity is a forbid den religion: Christians tolerated**. Death of Galeriu (May 311).

312 Edict of Toleration of Constantine and Licinius granting liberty to pagans and Christians. Victory of Constantine over Maxence at Milvan Bridge.

313 (February) Rescript of Milan, Constantine and of Liciniu granting liberty of worship to Christians and others Restitution of confiscated goods to Christians. **Christianit is put on an equal footing with other religions**.

324 Victory of Constantine over Licinius.

325 Council of Nicea (Ist Ecumenical Council) against the Arian heresy, called and presided over by Constantine (not yet baptized). Athanasius is the champion of ortho doxy.

330 Dedication of Constantinople as the imperial capital. I will become the capital of the Eastern Empire (Byzantine).

337 Baptism of Constantine on his deathbed by the Arian archbishop Eusebius of Nicomedia. Constans II favour Arianism

61- 63	**Julian restores pagan worship of Mithra**, said the *apostate* or the *philosopher*. Christians are again moderately persecuted but for a short time.
81	The Council of Constantinople reaffirms the censure of Arianism.
90	Ambrose, bishop of Milan, constrains Theodosius to a public humiliation by reason of the massacre of 7000 Thessalonians, following an uprising. For the first time an emperor submits to ecclesiastical authority.
91	Theodosius prohibits pagan worship in Rome and Alexandria and in 392 in all the Empire. **Christianity = State Religion**: it's the beginning of "Cesaropapism" or "Constantinian Christianity." The hereditary character of Christianity is reinforced. The pretended victory of Christianity is in reality a surrender of its original specific distinctives.
10	Capture of Rome by the Goths.

DIAGRAM OF GENERAL EVOLUTION OF BAPTISM AND BAPTISMAL INSTALLATIONS

Extract from the work of A. Khatchatrian: *Origin and Typology of Paleo-christian Baptisteries.*

Meaning of Baptism	Baptism-symbol of the union of the believer with Christ in His death and resurrection	Baptism-sacrament which blots out all sins		Baptism-sacrament which blots out original sin (Augustine)
Mode of Baptism	Total immersion of believers already regenerated		Total immersion of adults resulting in regeneration → Partial immersion of adults → Total immersion of children — Partial immersion of children (Ambrosian Rite) — Orthodox church → Affusion of adults, and later of infants		Groups of Baptist types
Baptismal Installations	Iˢᵗ to IVᵗʰ centuries No specific installation: living water, rivers, lakes, sea (Exception: Doura Europos)	IIⁿᵈ to IVᵗʰ cent. Existing Installations: Impluvium, thermal baths, private baths	IVᵗʰ to XIVᵗʰ centuries Constructed baptisteries - Baptismal pools in independent or separate buildings	VIIᵗʰ to XIVᵗʰ cent. Baptismal pools in churches	XVᵗʰ to XXᵗʰ cent. Baptismal fonts in churches

The pools come out of the ground and contain less and less water

Here is simply a general diagram and not a continued precise evolution. Certain forms which follow each other in the diagram are sometimes contemporaneous or even in reverse. The immersion of adults is proven up until the XIVᵗʰ century, whereas aspersion of adults or children already appear in the IIⁿᵈ century. Depending on the locality, practices differ during the same period. From the very first centuries dissident religious groups wanted to remain faithful to the apostolic model. Other religious groups beginning in the XVIᵗʰ century, and especially from the XVIIᵗʰ century onward strove to come back to the symbolic significance of total immer-

By total immersion (submersion)
Standing position
- bending of the body forward or backward
- bending of the knees forward or backward

Kneeling position:

By partial immersion – standing position
in water up to the ankles, the knees or to the waist / kneeling position: pour plenty of water over the head. (The *Didache*, around 120 A.D., allows affusion if immersion is impossible)

Sitting position: bending of the body backward

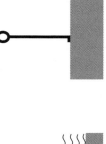

By affusion – standing position, kneeling or lying down (clinical baptism): a little water poured over the head.

INFANT BAPTISM

By total immersion horizontal

By total immersion vertical (Orthodox churches)

By partial immersion: (the head only, Ambrosian rite, province of Milan)

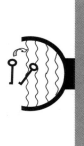

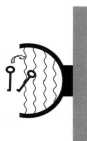

By affusion only: a little water poured over the head of the child (Catholic church, Protestant churches)

The **Biblical mode of baptism** is indisputably the total immersion of believers. This more exactly corresponds to the meaning of the Greek word: *baptizo* (βαπτίζω). It expresses most eloquently the baptismal symbol of the identification of the repentant and believing candidate with the death of Christ, His burial and His resurrection. This mode is in perfect harmony with the details mentioned in the descriptive texts of the first centuries (Acts 8:38, 39, etc.) and with the dimensions of the most ancient baptismal pools discovered by the archaeologists.

71

APPENDIX IV: THE EVOLUTION OF BAPTISM THROUGH THE CENTURIES

PERIOD	PREPARATION	AGENT	SUBJECT	INSTALLATION	CONDITION
Ist Century: **Church of the New Testament**	Nothing is indicated	Apostle, Elder, Bishop, Deacon (Philip)	Sinner repentant toward God and faith in Jesus Christ	No special installation Rivers, Ponds, Bath installations, etc.	Personal experience of conversion: repentance and faith. Change of mentality
IVth Century: **Towards a State Church**	40 days of teaching during Lent	Bishop (meaning between the bishop of the New Testament and the bishop of today)	Sinners converted or unconverted, adults or children	Large pools allowing total immersion of an adult	40 days of catechism
Later: **Catholic Church**	Preparation of the parents or godfathers and godmothers	Priest (or laymen in case of danger of death of the infant)	In general: unconscious infants	Small baptismal fonts appropriate for the affusion of a newborn	Parents or believing godparents
XVIth Century: **Reformation**	Preparation of the parents	Pastor	Chiefly infants	Baptismal fonts	Parents or believing godparents

REMARKS ON THE PRESENT SITUATION

In the New Testament, the baptism of the Spirit (new birth, regeneration) and water baptism (immersion) form an inseparable couple and even a unit: *One Lord, one faith, one baptism - Repent every one of you and be baptized...* Examples: the 3000 at Pentecost, the pagans at Cornelius' house, Saul of Tarsus, the Ethiopian eunuch, Lydia, the Philippian jailer.

Today, Christianity separates conversion from baptism, from whence arise five principal categories of "Christians" or situations:

1. In the unconverted churches:

    a) a deformed premature baptism (affusion of infants) followed by a conversion considerably delayed.

    b) a deformed baptism (affusion of infants) never followed by conversion. That is in the great majority of cases.

IGNIFI- ANCE	MODE	LOCALITY	TIME	SETTING	ADDED RITES	FORMULA EMPLOYED
ymbol: eath, urial nd esurrection ith Christ	Total immersion = burial under water	No special locality: in the open air, inside or outside of buildings without specific characteristics	No particular time. Almost immediately after the individual's conversion	Church of immersed believers (A professing church)	None	In the Name of the Lord or in the Name of the Father, Son and Holy Spirit
acrament: lots out ll sins, om /hence elayed aptism (cf. onstantine)	Triple immersion, range of partial immersion or affusion	Baptisteries built near churches	During the night of Easter and of Pentecost	In the church which was becoming a state church (church of unregene- rate and regenerate)	Blessing of the water, exorcism, anointing with oil, white vestments, laying on of hands	One is baptized in the Name of the Father, the Son and the Holy Spirit
acrament: lots out riginal sin: ence early aptism	Sprinkling, affusion, immersion in the Orthodox Church	Baptismal chapel in the church	Sundays	Mixed parish composed of believers and unbelievers	Blessing of the water anointing of Holy Oil lighted candles	"I baptize you in the Name of the Father and the Son and the Holy Spirit"
hannel of race ign of the ovenant of race	Generally affusion	In the church building	Especially on Sunday	Mixed parish	None	"I baptize you in the Name of the Father and of the Son and of the Holy Spirit"

2. In the professing churches:

) a conversion followed by a delayed biblical baptism;
) a conversion without subsequent baptism. In many cases, the converted consid-
r their infant baptism as valid and do not worry about biblical baptism. Are they
eal disciples, if they do not submit to the commands of the Lord and do not fol-
ow His example?
ortunately, there is a 5th category:
) regenerated persons, immersed on profession of faith, members of a biblical church.

73

For the reader wishing to learn more on the history of baptis
teries, we recommend the work of Dr. J. Volanakis: "Paleo
christian Baptisteries of Greece", Athens 1976.

APPENDIX V: SUMMARY OF THE WORK OF
Dr. J. VOLANAKIS

The work on *"The Paleo-christian Baptisteries of Greece"* dis
cusses the baptisteries of the Greek world known today. We
are sure that 52 of them are baptisteries, 18 very probably
served as such and two others are only certified by literary
documents.

This study is divided as follows:

1st section: Introduction

Chap. 1:   The administration of baptism in the East in
the paleo-christian period.

Chap. 2:   The Typology of paleo-christian baptisteries
in Greece.

Chap. 3:   The baptismal pools in Greece

2nd section: Descriptive catalogue of paleo-christian bap
tisteries in Greece: Peloponnesus, Central Greece
Thessalonica, Epire, Macedonia-Thrace, Isles of the
Aegean Sea, Cyclades, Dodecanese and Crete.

3rd section: Chronological catalogue; typology of baptismal pools; alphabetical index of first names, certified by
Greek inscriptions, used by Christians in the paleo-christian period; general index; plans and tables.

Here are the conclusions of this study:

1. During the first two centuries Christian baptism was prac-

tised in "living water"; that is to say, water from springs, rivers, lakes or the sea. Already, during the first half of the 3rd century, independent rooms are certified as baptisteries. Beginning at the second half of the 4th century, we find, in Greece, baptisteries built beside basilicas. Meanwhile, the most part were built in the 5th and 6th centuries.

2. In general the baptistery is composed of two parts: an anteroom in which the first part of the baptism took place, and beside it, a main part in which the baptismal pool is located and in which the second part of the baptism was accomplished. Sometimes a third part is found called "*consignatorium*", and further, more rarely a fourth part called "*catéchumenum*".

3. As to its location in relation to the church, the baptistery is generally located in proximity to the narthex, for it was reserved for the non baptized.

4. The plans of the Greek baptisteries show different types of construction. They are buildings of three naves, rectangular constructions, square, tetrahedral, cruciform or octagonal. Stones and ordinary mortar generally constitute the building materials. They are covered with a wooden ceiling or a cupola.

5. The baptismal pools are most often made of brick with waterproof mortar with marble facing. In general, they are found in the center of the main room in order to facilitate the movement of the neophytes around the pool. A few monolithic baptismal pools are dated in the 6th century and constitute a preparatory transition to the baptismal fonts of the Middle Ages.

6. The baptismal pools have different shapes: they are cruciform, round, square, octagonal and hexagonal. The baptismal fonts are cylindrical or cruciform.

7. In the beginning the practice of baptism was very simple Little by little, it takes on a more elaborate liturgy Different liturgical types come into being. In Greece baptism was administered in the Byzantium mode. The baptism was always linked to the liturgy of the first communion of the neophytes.

8. Confirmation followed immediately upon baptism for which they used the *"chrismarium"* or *"consignatorium"*. Ablution soon followed.

9. Baptism was administered by a triple submersion and immersion, which is evident by the depth, width and general shape of the baptismal pool. Liturgical texts and others further certify this practice. Both adult and infant baptism were practised. Since the end of the 6th or the beginning of the 7th century, infant baptism is predominant. For this reason, the baptistery as a separate room is eliminated and replaced by baptismal fonts.

10. During the first three centuries in Greece Christianity did not develop very much. Since the 4th and especially since the 5th and 6th centuries nearly all the inhabitants of Greece were baptized and incorporated into Christianity.

11. The resemblances that one can observe between the Greek baptisteries and those of Eastern countries (Asia Minor, Syria, Palestine) can be explained by the ecclesiastical, political and cultural relations existing among these countries. The common aspects among the baptisteries of the paleo-christian Christianity demonstrate a relative unity in paleo-christian art in spite of the particularities which may be explained by local traditions.

12. The greater part of Greek baptisteries were destroyed by the Barbaric Invasions of the 7th and 8th centuries as well as by earthquakes, fires, etc. The baptisteries of the Dodecanese are the best preserved, but a goodly number of baptisteries are still waiting to be the object of archaeological research.

We are grateful for this testimony of a specialist witness.

APPENDIX VI

FROM THE BIBLICAL CHURCH TO MODERN APOSTASY

"How pure gold changed into base lead?" (Racine)

New tendencies to primitive Christianity are already manifested in the bosom of the apostolic churches. The apostle Paul must wrestle against the influence of Jewish legalism (the importance of works in salvation) and against the influence of philosophy (vain and dangerous speculations of the intellect: Gnosticism).

Materialization:

→ from symbol to sacrament

The inner spiritual reality represented by an outward sign in the case of baptism and the Lord's Supper is hardly perceptible, but almost entirely, replaced by the sign. That which was only a symbol becomes a sacrament. Then following certain practices, other sacraments appear. Finally the Council of Trent (1545-1563) fixed the number to seven: baptism, confirmation, the Eucharist (former communion), penance, extreme unction, holy orders, and matrimony. These ceremonies no longer symbolize grace already received but confer grace. The acts themselves become meritorious and exercise a magical power independently of the dispositions of the heart and mind.

Clericalization:

> from the initial brotherhood to organized hierarchy

Christians withdraw from well-known and primitive brotherhood. To administer the sacraments, you need specialists, the elders become bishops, and other functions are instituted. A hierarchy is established and the bishop of Rome becomes the supreme head of the churches. The ordinary faithful are finally dependent on human intermediaries to make peace with God. The unique mediation of Jesus Christ is replaced by the mediation of the clergy, the saints and the virgin. The clergy is a special class recognized by their clothes. Holy Orders is a sacrament. Apostolic succession no longer rests on being faithful to the teaching of the apostles but in the transmission of power from the present clergy to the clergy of tomorrow. The ecclesiastical authority is asserted: the use of force and physical constraint spreads more and more in the repression of heresy (considered rightly or wrongly).

Defining of doctrine:

> from divine revelation to human inventions

In the face of Jewish and pagan adversaries and before the blossoming of heresies, Christianity must define its doctrine. Christians attempt to systematize. Great controversies take place and councils are called upon to make decisions. The Bible no longer suffices as a doctrinal source. One progressively adds tradition (Church Fathers, Council Decrees, Pontifical Dogmas). This tradition possesses the same authority as the Bible (*Council of Trent*). In fact it is considered to be superior to the Scriptures, for it gives the true interpretation thereof. From all this evolution, a system of human inspiration is born, if not diabolical, then doctrine generally foreign and often contrary to the teachings of the Bible. Ecclesiastical authority today pretends to be the sole interpreter of Scripture and to teach the truth.

Universalism:

→ from the biblical church (*ecclesia*) to the unregenerate church

By the development of the sacraments, in which the outward act alone suffices (if not in doctrine at least in practice), the difference between the churches and the world is blurred and disappears. One no longer becomes a Christian through the new birth, but one is born a Christian or one becomes one through infant baptism. Also, one must not be surprised at the recognition of Christianity as a State religion (under Theodosius in 391) and the resulting consequences. All the citizens of the empire are thus Christians, at least by name. Christianity has become hereditary. Babies are received into the church by "baptismal regeneration". The professing churches are replaced by unregenerate churches. These societies of Christians in name only are no longer "churches" in the biblical meaning of the term.

Localization:

→ of worship in spirit and in truth to manifestations localized in space and time

As under the ancient Covenant one worshiped in Jerusalem, at the same time, imperceptibly, one worships in the area consecrated for worship. As before, also, one worships more especially at certain times. Feast days are instituted; their dates are fixed in one way or another. There is an ecclesiastical calendar. Pagan festivals are given "Christian" content. But at the same time these festivals reveal the paganism of natural man. The theory of holy sites and consecrated times permit the "faithful" to have times and locations where they escape from divine requirements.

Humanization:

→ from the condescension of God to the exaltation of man

The incarnation and death of the Son was the most explosive manifestation of the condescension of God with respect to His defiled and rebellious creatures. But the resurrected Christ has been sovereignly exalted. The worship and missionary activity of the primitive church are for the glory of God and of His Son. Man is as nothing before his Creator and his Redeemer. Without realising we evolve toward the exaltation of man. The priests and dignitaries of the "Church" abrogate to themselves that which belongs only to God. The creature is glorified even to calling the Bishop of Rome "Holy Father" and in the case of Mary "Queen of Heaven". In other realms we celebrate the conquests of "Science" or we hope for the combined efforts of men (Liberalism, Ecumenism) the Kingdom of God on earth, a golden age of peace and universal prosperity.

Paganization:

→ from primitive Christianity to a pagan-Christian system

The sum total of these tendencies brings Christianity to the level of a pagan religion. Magic practices, centralized organization, the use of force, human traditions, the localizing of worship are traces whose origins go back to pagan practices or to Judaism, or to civil and religious administration of the Roman Empire. In becoming earthy, human and temporal, Christianity loses its spiritual characteristics, divine and eternal, which it originally possessed. This strange and diabolical association of Christianity with paganism resulted in the birth of the great Roman Catholic movements or Orthodox, Anglican or reformed, in which, in spite of the deviations of their system, true worshipers worship God in spirit and in truth; while in communities in which the religious system is more conformable to the primitive ideal, some individual believers manifest, in varying degrees, this same pagan-Christian union by their doctrinal errors or their disordered Christian life. That explains the constant, unwarranted interference of the old pagan nature in all the realms of the spiritual life of true believers.

This is why this word applies to all: *"Watch and Pray"*.

"Remember therefore from whence thou art fallen, and repent, and do the first works".   Revelation 2:5

APPENDIX VII

DESCRIPTION OF A BAPTISMAL CEREMONY BY CYRIL OF JERUSALEM ABOUT 350 AD

At a certain time one is made aware of a curious rite of expectorating. The neophyte had to spit toward the West, where symbolically the demon lived.

An interesting text of Cyril of Jerusalem (315-386) permits us to be present at a baptismal ceremony in the middle of the 4th century (347-350):

"As soon as you enter the interior of the building (the baptistery) you take off your tunic, signifying the casting off of the old man and his practices. Stripped, you are naked, thus imitating in that also the Christ, naked on the cross, which, by his nakedness cast off the principalities and powers and boldly dragged on the wood in his triumphant cortège. Once stripped, you are anointed with exorcised oil, from the top of the hair of the head to the feet. You thus become a participant of the true olive tree, Jesus Christ. Detached indeed from the wild olive tree you are grafted on the true olive tree, participating in its fruitfulness. After that you are led by the hand, into the pool of God's baptism, like Christ, from the cross to the grave which is before you. Each one is asked if you believe in the Father, in the Son and in the Spirit. You confess saving faith. Then you are immersed three times in the water and you come up out of the water, thus signifying symbolically the burial of three days of the Lord. For just as our Saviour stayed three days and three nights in the heart of the earth, so also, you too, in coming out for the first time, you represented the first day that Christ passed on earth and in replunging yourself in the water, the night which followed it. Just as the one who is in the night sees no more, whereas the one who is in the day lives in full light, just

as during your immersion, as in the night, you see nothing, but in your coming out of the water, you find yourself in full day. In like manner you die and you are born in the same moment and that holy water served you at the same time as a tomb and a mother. And that which Solomon said in another connection can be well applied to you: There is, he said, a time to be born and a time to die. For you, in reverse, there is a time to die and a time to be born: a single instant operated the one and the other and your birth coincided with your death."

(IInd *Mystagogique Catechism*, 2-4)

This detailed description of baptismal practice from the middle of the 4th century calls for a few remarks:

- The candidates are still adults, as originally. They are conscious: they answer the questions. They confess at least theoretically, the Christian faith.

- The baptism, further, is done by immersion, and even by triple immersion (practised by the orthodox church, though it applies there to infants).

- Cyril speaks of a "holy water" which implicates already the sacramentary character of baptism, keeping in mind, besides, the symbolic character of death with Christ, and of birth to new life (resurrection with Christ, Romans 6:3-11).

- Subsequently, the symbol will make way for sacrament essentially for infants, resulting in the shrinking of baptismal pools.

GLOSSARY

Affusion
Procedure which consists of pouring water on one part of the body. Synonym: effusion, infusion. To distinguish from sprinkling where the water does not flow.

Aspersion
Liquid (water) sprinkled by drops on someone.

Baptistery
Designates the building sheltering the baptismal installation and not the pool or fonts.

Basilica
Civil or religious building divided into several parallel naves.
Christian church of Early Middle Ages built on the plan of the civic basilicas.

Capitulary[44]
Order of a Frankish King or Emperor.

Central Plan
A building stretching around a center like a rotunda or a polygon with at least five sides.

Church
From *ek kaleo* = to call out.
Three cases in Acts 19:25, 32, 39 with a common, profane or judicial meaning (a gathering, a corporation, a specialized assembly).
Narrow Christian meaning: believers chosen to constitute a group of Christians = a local church ("church of Corinth"); Acts 11:22 (this reference refers to Antioch).
Broader Christian meaning: Ecclesiastical Christian organization. For example: the Roman Catholic Church, the history of the Church.

Clinic
Which is practised on the bed-ridden (clinical baptism).

Codex
A text bound like book and not a scroll.

Collegiality
Power exercised by several persons of the same authority.

Congregational
Administration not by an individual but by the gathered congregation.

Conversion
To pass from a belief considered false (pagan) to the assumed truth. Conversion to Christianity = to pass by repentance to faith in adopting Christian

---

[4] Relating to an ecclesiastical chapter.

	teaching and practice. The term finally signifie(simply a change of religion.
Edict	Statute published by the emperor or magistrate.
Effusion	Act of pouring a liquid out of a container.
Exegete	from exegesis = interpretation of Scripture, inter preter of the meaning of a text.
Gothic	Posterior to the Roman Period (XIIth to XVIth cen turies).
Harmonization	Put texts in agreement with others.
Iconography	The science of the representations of themes, sym bols, or personages.
Immersion	The act of plunging in a liquid. It may be partial o total. In the latter case, it is "submersion".
Lesson	Reading, variant, text as it appears in a manuscrip
Limes	Border of the Roman Empire. We distinguish th Rhenan borders and the Danube borders.
Narthex	Vestibule of a religious building distinct from th exterior porch or entrance proper.
Neophyte	Person newly converted to Christianity.
Paleo-christian	From the period of the first Christians to the mid dle of the VIth century.
Paedobaptist	One who practises infant baptism (paedo-baptism)
Pre Roman	Prior to the Roman period which begins in the IX^t century.
Priesthood	Ministry of the pope and bishops, and simpl priests. It implies authority and a spiritual powe indispensable for administering the sacraments.
Rescript	Answers from the Emperor to questions asked b the magistrates or the governors of the provinces To distinguish from an edict (cf. Edict of Galère o 311 and the Rescript of Milan of 313).
Sacrament	Sacred act or object. A rite which produces o increases grace for souls. The Council of Tren (1545-1565) defines them and limits them to seven baptism, confirmation, eucharist, extreme unction matrimony, holy orders and penance. They ar quasi-magic acts, which function by themselves independently of the priest who confers them, an of the person benefiting from them. Baptism which originally was only a symbol became sacrament when the "elder" became a "priest

invested with special powers. In the Church in the second century sacraments were not always available everywhere.

ola fide — By faith alone.

ola gratia — By grace alone.

ubmersion — Total immersion.

ymbol — The conventional representation of an abstract operation involving a person, object, act, etc. Baptism by immersion is the symbol of the burial and resurrection with Christ. Baptism which has a symbolic meaning became a sacrament by the "sacerdotal" powers of the priest.

extual Criticism — Is distinguished from Higher Criticism or historic or literary criticism. Textual Criticism endeavors to reconstitute the original text.

Bibliography

Atlas des monuments paléochretiens de France

- **Naissance des arts chrétiens**   1991

- **Les premiers monuments chrétiens de France:**

        - *1. Sud-Est et Corse*   1995
        - *2. Sud-Ouest et Centre*   1996
        - *3. Nord-Ouest et Est*   1998

Picard, Paris

De Boccard	*Topographie chrétienne des cités de la Gaule de origines au milieu du VIIIe siècle*
F. Buhler	**Occupation Romaine des Régions Rhénanes et questions posées par les Installations Baptismale dans les Ouvrages Militaires** Musée historique, Mulhouse 1984
A. Khatchatrian	*Les Baptistères Paléochrétiens* Klincksieck, Paris 1962
A. Khatchatrian	*Origine et Typologie des Baptistères Paléochrétiens* Centre de Culture Chrétienne, Mulhouse 1982
G. Moracchini Mazel	*Les Monuments Paléochrétiens de Corse* Klincksieck, Paris 1967
Jean Guyon	*Les Premiers Baptistères des Gaules (IVe-VIIIe siècles)* Unione Internazionale Degli Istituti di Archeologia Storia e Storia dell'Arte in Roma, Rome 2000
F. Buhler	*Beitrag der Archäologie zur Frage der Taufe* Fundamentum, FETA, Basel 1987
F. Buhler	*L'Eglise Locale, un Manuel Pratique* Farel 1985
J.G. Davies	*The Architectural Setting of Baptism*, London, 1962